I Belong to the Sikh Faith

Katie Dicker and Amar Singh Perihar

PowerKiDS press.

New York

Published in 2010 by The Rosen Publishing Group Inc.
29 East 21st Street, New York, NY 10010

First Edition

Library of Congress Cataloging-in-Publication Data

Dicker, Katie.
  I belong to the Sikh faith / Katie Dicker and Amar Singh Perihar.
    p. cm. -- (I belong)
  Includes index.
  ISBN 978-1-4358-3036-3 (library binding)
  ISBN 978-1-4358-8626-1 (paperback)
  ISBN 978-1-4358-8627-8 (6-pack)
  1. Religious life--Sikhism--Juvenile literature. I. Perihar, Amar Singh. II. Title.
  BL2018.37.D53 2010
  294.6--dc22

                          2008051879

Manufactured in China

Disclaimer
The text in this book is based on the experience of one family. Although every effort
has been made to offer accurate and clearly expressed information, the author and
publisher acknowledge that some explanations may not be relevant to those who
practice their faith in a different way.

Acknowledgements
The author and publisher would like to thank the following people for their help and
participation in this book:
The Perihar family, Bindu Rai, Ranjit Kaur Khaira, and Pavinder Singh Garcha.

Photography by Chris Fairclough.

Contents

My family

Hi, I'm Amar, and this is my family—my mom and dad and my sister, Hera. We're Sikhs. Today it's Sunday and we're going to the **gurdwara**.

The gurdwara is open every day, but we go on the weekend when we're off of school and Mom and Dad are off of work.

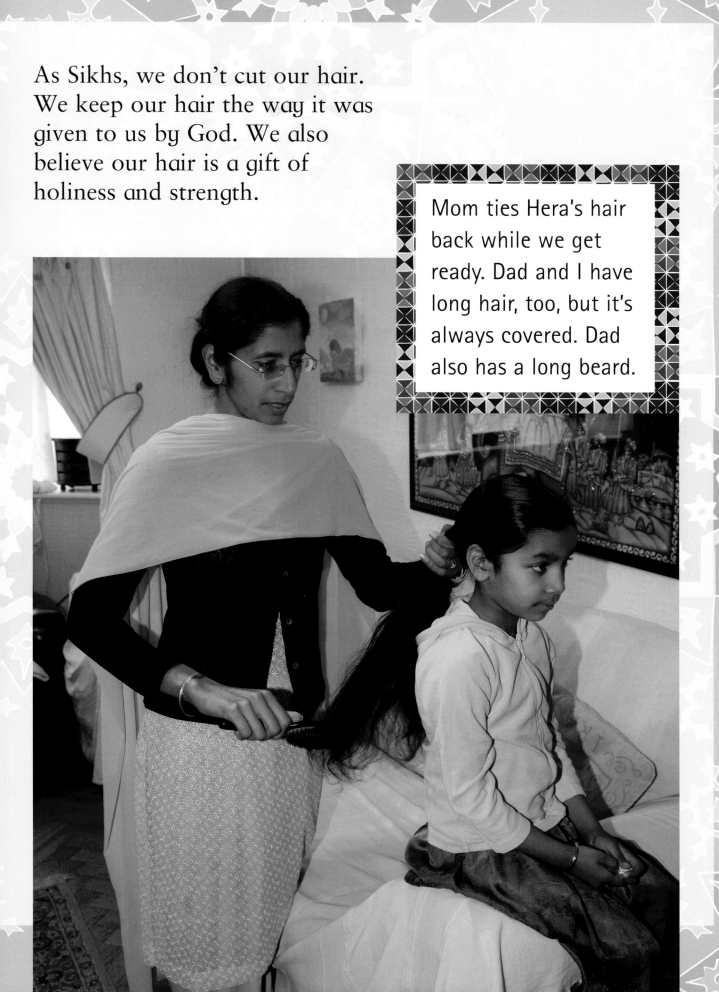

As Sikhs, we don't cut our hair. We keep our hair the way it was given to us by God. We also believe our hair is a gift of holiness and strength.

Mom ties Hera's hair back while we get ready. Dad and I have long hair, too, but it's always covered. Dad also has a long beard.

The five Ks

When Sikhs choose to receive **amrit**, they wear the **five Ks**. They do not remove hair from their bodies. They wear a steel bracelet and cotton shorts as underwear, and they carry a comb and a small sword.

Dad wears a **turban**—the material is 16 feet long! I wear a **patka** but when I'm older, I'll wear a turban, too.

The comb reminds us to keep our lives in order, the small sword is a sign that we must stand up for people in need, and the cotton shorts are for **modesty**. The bracelet reminds us that God has no beginning or end.

Dad shows me the five Ks. I have long hair and I wear a steel bracelet, but when I'm older, I hope I am blessed with the gift of amrit and wear all five Ks.

Who were the gurus?

Sikhism was started by a man named Guru Nanak Dev Ji, who lived in India about 600 years ago. He taught people that there is only one true God and showed them how to live a good life.

This picture reminds me of Guru Gobind Singh Ji (left) and Guru Nanak Dev Ji (right), the last and first gurus. The gurus were teachers and warriors.

God's widsom passed from Guru Nanak Dev Ji to nine other gurus. The tenth guru, Guru Gobind Singh Ji, made our holy book, the **Guru Granth Sahib**, about 300 years ago. This became the **eternal** guru when he died.

The gurus' teachings have passed through many generations. The Sikhs we meet at the gurdwara share their love and support with us.

At the gurdwara

The gurdwara is open to everyone, whatever their background. Upstairs there's a prayer hall and some classrooms, and downstairs is a kitchen and a hall where we eat.

We often wear traditional clothes at the gurdwara. Mom and Hera wear a **salwar kameez** and I wear a **kurta pajama**.

When we get inside, we take off our shoes and cover our heads to show our respect. We also wash our hands before we go to the prayer hall. This is a large room where the holy book is kept.

We bow down and look toward the Guru Granth Sahib whenever we can. Covering our head reminds us that the hand of God is over us.

The Guru Granth Sahib

The Guru Granth Sahib is our guide to life—the eternal guru. A copy of the book is kept on a large throne, surrounded by special cloths called rumulas. The holy book is covered by these cloths after a service.

This lady is called a **granthi**. During the service, she reads the holy book aloud. Both men and women can become a granthi.

The holy book is full of the gurus' teachings about living a good and honest life. But it contains words of wisdom from other faiths, too. The gurus taught us how important it is to respect other religions.

A fan called a chaur is used to keep the area around the holy book clean. The chaur is traditionally made from horsehair.

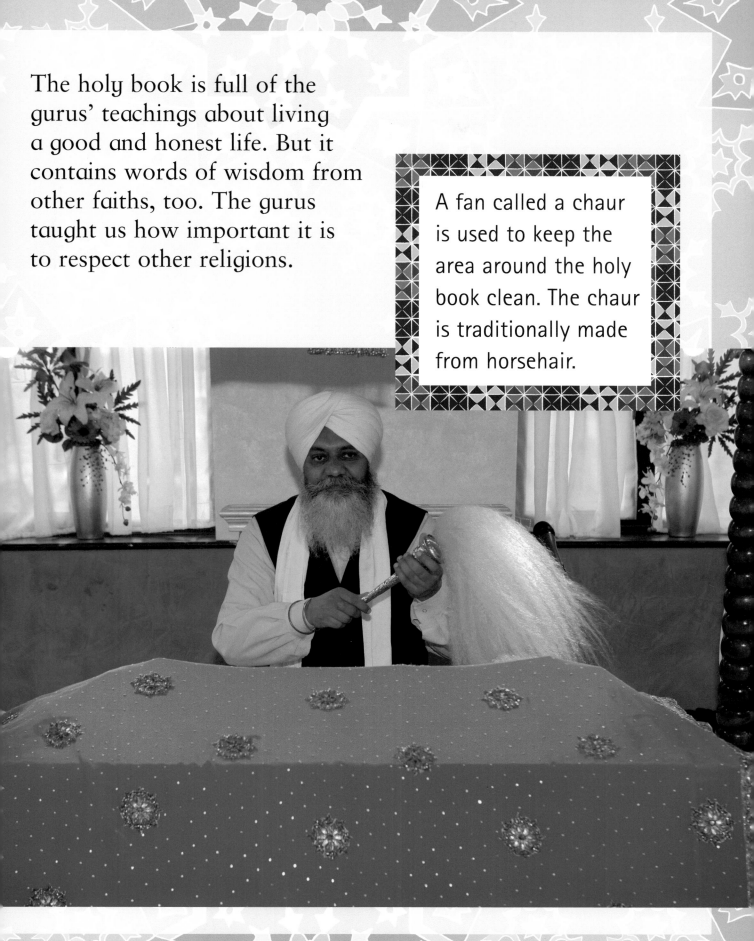

How do we worship?

We listen to **kirtan** and sing hymns called shabads when we worship. The **raghis** also sing verses from the holy book and explain their meaning as they sing.

The raghis are playing drums called tablas and a type of harmonium called a baja. I would love to learn to play like them!

At the end of the service, we say special prayers called Ardas. We praise God and we ask for his help and support in our lives. We all stand facing the Guru Granth Sahib and close our eyes as we pray.

After the Ardas, we receive this sweet food called **Karah Prasad**. It is given to show that we are all equal in the eyes of God.

The langar

At the gurdwara, we share a meal called a langar after the service. As Sikhs, it's important to share what we have. The first guru taught that God loves us all. He invited all people to eat together, whoever they were.

There's a big kitchen at the gurdwara. I'm helping to make some vegetable curry for everyone to eat—it looks very tasty!

We all help at the gurdwara—
we're like one big family. Some
people bring food or offer
money toward the meal, and
others clean and cook. We also
make vegetarian food so that
everyone can eat.

We all sit on the floor
and eat together. After
our meal, we catch up
with friends—and make
new friends, too!

Learning at the gurdwara

On the weekends, Hera and I go to classes at the gurdwara. We find out more about the Sikh way of life and we learn **Punjabi**. We meet a lot of our friends at the classes, too.

The gurus taught us to work hard. Today we're learning about festivals, such as **Vaisakhi**, that are linked to the lives of the gurus.

The verses of the holy book are written in **Gurmukhi,** the Punjabi script. *Gurmukhi* means "from the mouth of the guru." We learn Punjabi so we can read the gurus' teachings for ourselves.

I love trying to write the Punjabi alphabet. I try to practice whenever I can. There are 35 letters and special symbols, too.

Living a Sikh life

The gurus taught us to share our things—and our time—with others. They also taught us to pray whenever we can throughout the day, to thank God for all the good things he has given us.

When I pray, I also think about the way I behave. I use these prayer beads to help me concentrate on the words I am saying.

The teachings of the gurus show me how to be a good person. I try to work hard, to be kind to other people, and to be honest. I am proud to be a Sikh.

Hera's a year younger than me. She's a good friend as well as my sister. We try to help each other in all that we do.

Glossary, further information, and Web Sites

amrit a baptism ceremony for Sikhs.

eternal something that lasts forever.

granthi someone who reads the Guru Granth Sahib aloud during a Sikh service.

gurdwara a place where Sikhs go to worship God.

Gurmukhi an alphabet written by the second guru as part of the Punjabi language.

Guru Granth Sahib a holy book for Sikhs (the eternal guru). Also known as Adi Granth.

Karah Prasad a sweet food made from flour, butter, and sugar, given out after a Sikh service.

kirtan hymns sung from the Guru Granth Sahib.

kurta pyjama a tunic and pants.

modesty to dress in a way that does not show off parts of the body.

patka a cloth head covering worn by some Sikh children.

Punjabi a language originally from parts of India and Pakistan.

raghis skilled musicians who perform at a gurdwara.

salwar kameez a pair of pants and a loose shirt.

Sikhism the Sikh religion.

turban a single piece of cloth, tied around the head.

Did you know?

- *Sikh* means "learner."
- There are around 20 million Sikhs in the world, mostly living in India.
- Some Sikh festivals are called gurpurbs. They celebrate days in the lives of the gurus.

Activities

1. Do you know any gurpurbs? Use books or the internet to find out what they are about.
2. Find the Gurmukhi alphabet using books or the internet. Can you write your name in Gurmukhi?
3. Write a poem about the Sikh way of life.

Books to read

- *This is my Faith: Sikhism*
  by Anita Ganeri
  (Barron's Educational, 2006)

- *Traditional Religious Tales:*
  Sikh Stories
  by Anita Ganeri
  (Picture Window Books, 2006)

- *World Religions: Sikhism*
  by Joy Barrow
  (Walrus Books, 2005)

Web Sites

Due to the changing nature of Internet links, PowerKids Press has developed an online list of Web sites related to the subject of this book. This site is updated regularly. Please use this link to access this list: www.powerkidslinks.com/blong/sikh

Sikh festivals

Vaisakhi (April 13)
The Sikh New Year festival. This is also a reminder of the day that Guru Gobind Singh Ji created the Khalsa (or Sikh community).

Birth of Guru Arjan Dev Ji (May 2)
A celebration of the birthday of the fifth guru.

Bandi Chor Divas (Diwali) (Oct./Nov.)
The festival of light celebrating the day the sixth guru was released from captivity.

Birth of Guru Nanak Dev Ji (November)
Celebration of the birthday of the first guru.

Birth of Guru Gobind Singh Ji (January 5)
Celebration of the birthday of the tenth guru.

Hola Mohalla (February/March)
A festival when Sikhs practice military exercise and hold mock battles.

Sikh symbols

Five Ks Five symbols that baptized Sikhs wear. They are Kesh (uncut hair), Kanga (comb), Kara (steel bracelet), Kirpan (sword), and Kaccha (shorts).

Ik Oankar A symbol to show there is one God who rules over everything in the world.

Nishan Sahib An orange flag flown outside the gurdwara to show the building is a holy place for Sikhs.

Index